MW01504161

INSPIRATIONAL SHORT SPORT STORIES FOR YOUNG RISING ACHIEVERS

HOW 13 WORLD CLASS ATHLETES OVERCAME ADVERSITY TO ACHIEVE EXCELLENCE

ELVIN CREATIONS

© **Copyright Elvin Creations 2023 – All rights reserved.**

The content contained within this book may not be reproduced, duplicated or transmitted without direct written permission from the author or the publisher.

Under no circumstances will any blame or legal responsibility be held against the publisher, or author, for any damages, reparation, or monetary loss due to the information contained within this book. Either directly or indirectly. You are responsible for your own choices, actions, and results.

Legal Notice:

This book is copyright protected. This book is only for personal use. You cannot amend, distribute, sell, use, quote or paraphrase any part, or the content within this book, without the consent of the author or publisher.

Disclaimer Notice:

Please note the information contained within this document is for educational and entertainment purposes only. All effort has been executed to present accurate, up-to-date, and reliable, complete information. No warranties of any kind are declared or implied. Readers acknowledge that the author is not engaging in the rendering of legal, financial, medical or professional advice. The content within this book has been derived from various sources. Please consult a licensed professional before attempting any techniques outlined in this book.

By reading this document, the reader agrees that under no circumstances is the author responsible for any losses, direct or indirect, which are incurred as a result of the use of the information contained within this document, including, but not limited to—errors, omissions, or inaccuracies

CONTENTS

INTRODUCTION

In a society filled with innumerable diversions and obstacles, the path to excellence might appear intimidating. The road to success is rarely a straight line, and setbacks and barriers might feel overwhelming at times. However, within everyone of us is the potential for greatness, just waiting to be awakened by inspiration, effort, and unflinching belief.

Welcome to a trip that will take you through the lives and tales of some of the world's greatest athletes. This book is more than simply a compilation of sports stories; it is a source of inspiration, a source of motivation, and a testament to the amazing heights that young athletes and adolescent achievers like you may attain. As you read the pages, you will uncover the incredible adventures of people who began as dreamers and rose to become champions. Their stories represent not just their physical talent, but also their tenacious spirit, tenacity, and unwavering pursuit of perfection. These sportsmen have overcome adversity, overcome self-doubt, and become legendary in their respective sports.

This book, however, is about more than their victories on the field or court; it is about the values, beliefs, and life lessons that have defined their character. It is because of their efforts, discipline, and commitment that they have reached the peak of achievement. It's about their capacity to inspire, encourage, and act as role models for young athletes and achievers like you. Whether you are an aspiring athlete, an aspiring artist, a prospective scientist, or just someone with a goal, the stories in these pages will remind you that you have the ability to accomplish greatness. They will motivate you to pursue your ambitions with zeal, to endure in the face of hardship, and to believe in your heart's limitless potential. Remember, greatness is not reserved for the few; it is within the reach of anybody who dares to dream, believes in themselves, and is prepared to put in the hard work and devotion necessary to make their ambitions a reality. So, let these stories be your guiding light, source of encouragement, and reminder that you, too, are capable of greatness.

1

MICHAEL JORDAN

"I can accept failure, everyone fails at something. But I can't accept not trying."

From Childhood Aspirations to Air Jordan:

Michael Jeffrey Jordan was born in the tranquil town of Wilmington, North Carolina, in the early 1960s. Little did anybody realize that this boy would grow on to become one of the greatest players of all time, revolutionize basketball, and inspire millions with his relentless dedication and indomitable spirit.

Michael's family, notably his parents, James and Deloris Jordan, molded his boyhood. His father, James, worked at a GE factory, while his mother, Deloris, worked in a bank. They instilled in young Michael the principles of tenacity, discipline, and hard work. They had no idea that these ideals would lay the groundwork for his future success.

Michael has a strong interest in sports from a young age. He was a baseball, football, and basketball player. His real potential began to emerge on the basketball floor. Larry, his elder brother, frequently challenged him to one-on-one games, instilling a competitive spirit in young Michael. Michael, despite being the youngest sibling, refused to be surpassed, improving his abilities with an unwavering work ethic.

Michael's prowess on the basketball court was obvious to those who saw him play in high school. He went to

Emsley A. Laney High School, where he swiftly advanced through the junior varsity and varsity basketball levels. During his sophomore year, though, he was cut from the varsity squad, which was a setback. Instead of becoming discouraged, Jordan utilized his disappointment as fire to enhance his talents. He put in many hours of practice time, desperate to succeed.

Michael reached the varsity squad the next year and averaged an astounding 25 points per game. His tremendous work ethic and tenacity drew the attention of college scouts from all around the country. He received a basketball scholarship at the University of North Carolina in 1981, where he would refine his abilities and prepare for the next level of competition.

Jordan's brilliance shone brightly throughout his time at North Carolina. In 1982, he led the Tar Heels to an NCAA title, making the game-winning shot in the finals. His experience in college not only cemented his position as a basketball wonder, but it also taught him crucial lessons about cooperation and leadership that he would use in the future.

Jordan made the difficult choice to forego his final year at North Carolina and enter the NBA Draft in 1984 after three good years there. The Chicago Bulls picked him as the third overall choice, altering the direction of both his life and the franchise's history.

Jordan had a tremendous debut season with the Bulls. He averaged an astounding 28.2 points per game and was named NBA Rookie of the Year. His agility, talent, and competitive drive made him an overnight phenomenon. Fans all throughout the NBA admired his gravity-defying dunks, garnering him the moniker "Air Jordan."

Jordan endured his fair share of hurdles and failures as his career progressed. He had to deal with injuries, playoff setbacks, and naysayers who questioned his ability to lead a team to an NBA title. Jordan's genuine spirit and determination, however, emerged most in these times of difficulty.

Jordan led the Chicago Bulls to their first NBA title in 1991, after seven years in the league. It was a triumphant and vindicated moment, the product of years of hard work and dedication. The Bulls would go on to win two more championships in a row in 1992 and 1993, cementing Jordan's place as one of the greatest basketball players of all time.

Despite his remarkable success, Michael Jordan startled the basketball world by retiring in 1993. Personal grief and a desire to pursue other interests motivated his choice. Jordan spent his time away from the game pursuing a career in professional baseball, a sport he had loved since he was a youngster. Though his baseball career was brief, it proved his relentless dedication to taking on new challenges.

Jordan triumphantly returned to the NBA and the Chicago Bulls in 1995. His return was hailed with great expectation and enthusiasm from people all across the world. Jordan's homecoming coincided with the debut of the famed Air Jordan XI sneakers, demonstrating his long-lasting influence on sports and popular culture.

From 1996 through 1998, the Bulls won three more championships in a row, rounding off an unmatched era of supremacy. Jordan's leadership, scoring ability, and competitive spirit were unparalleled, winning him the NBA Finals MVP award each time.

Michael Jordan announced his retirement from basketball for the second time in 1999, leaving behind a legacy that transcended the sport itself. His influence stretched beyond the court, motivating a new generation of athletes and spectators to follow their aspirations with tenacity.

Jordan's narrative, however, did not end there. He made a return with the Washington Wizards in 2001, confounding expectations once more. Even in his latter years, he showed bursts of brilliance that reminded the world why he was regarded as the greatest of all time.

Jordan's influence stretched beyond basketball into business and philanthropy. He became a successful businessman, founding the Jordan Brand under Nike, which has now grown into a multibillion-dollar company. His charity contributions have included funding for education, children's hospitals, and disaster assistance.

Michael Jordan has demonstrated the strength of tenacity, dedication, and resilience throughout his life. Through persistent commitment to his work, he overcame setbacks, defied expectations, and attained greatness. His narrative reminds us that with enthusiasm and hard effort, we can overcome obstacles and achieve the remarkable.

What did we take away from him?

IIe taught us that failure is but a stepping stone to success, and he encouraged perseverance in the face of adversity. Jordan's unwavering rivalry motivated us to strive for greatness at all times, and his leadership exemplified the need of teamwork and collaboration. His inspirational comebacks proved that it is never too late to achieve our dreams. Jordan's global impact grew beyond our core businesses to branding and marketing, demonstrating the ability to leave a lasting legacy outside of our principal undertakings. Above all, he inspires us to believe in ourselves and give back to our communities, exhibiting the tenacity of the human spirit.

"If you do the work, you get rewarded. There are no shortcuts in life."

2

BABE RUTH

"Heroes get remembered, but legends never die."

B abe Ruth, who was born in 1895, is best
remembered as a baseball icon and one of the
sport's greatest power hitters. Originally a pitcher for
the Boston Red Sox, he rose to prominence as a home
run hitter with the New York Yankees. Ruth established
multiple records, including the legendary 60 home runs

in a single season in 1927. His massive home runs earned him the moniker "The Sultan of Swat." Ruth's captivating demeanor and popularity made him a cultural figure of the Roaring Twenties outside of baseball. His long reputation as a symbol of American sports success continues to attract baseball fans and aficionados throughout the world.

From a Lowly Beginning to a Baseball Legend:

George Herman Ruth Sr. and Kate Schamberger Ruth had a newborn boy in the early hours of February 6, 1895, in a working-class area of Baltimore, Maryland. They had no idea that their kid, George Herman Ruth Jr., would grow up to become one of baseball's most iconic personalities and a lasting emblem of the American ideal.

George Jr., who would eventually be known as "Babe Ruth," had a difficult upbringing. His parents were poor, and living in the Ruth family was far from luxury. Babe's parents tried their best to care for their family with minimal finances, but they quickly recognized that their kid was a handful. Babe was notorious for his wild antics and mischievous nature, which frequently landed him into trouble.

His parents took the difficult decision to send him to St. Mary's Industrial School for Boys, a Catholic reform school and orphanage in Baltimore, when he was seven years old. Babe's life changed dramatically at this point. One of the school's caregivers, Brother Matthias, spotted Babe's ability and introduced him to baseball. Babe began to hone his baseball talents under the tutelage of Brother Matthias. He shown a tremendous talent for the sport, immediately becoming a prominent player among the school's lads. Baseball became more than a pastime to Babe; it became a lifeline—a chance for him to escape the difficulties of his childhood and dream of a better future.

While honing his baseball skills, Babe drew the notice of Jack Dunn, owner of the Baltimore Orioles, a minor league baseball team. baby Ruth earned his first professional contract with the Orioles when he was 19 years old. Dunn recognized potential in Babe and famously referred to him as "my new babe," earning the moniker that would cling with him for life. Babe Ruth's tenure with the Orioles was brief. He was sold to the Boston Red Sox in 1914, beginning his Major League Baseball (MLB) career. Babe Ruth's reputation as a brilliant pitcher began to cement with the Red Sox. He was well-known for his strong left arm and ability to strike out hitters. Babe's adventure, however, was about to take another unexpected turn. The Boston Red Sox controversially sold Babe Ruth to the New York Yankees in 1919. This move would go on to become one of the most famous and influential transactions in baseball history.

Babe Ruth evolved from a pitcher to a power-hitting outfielder with the Yankees. His amazing ability to hit home runs captivated spectators and changed baseball into a more thrilling and high-scoring sport. He broke and set records by hitting an astonishing 60 home runs in a single season in 1927, a number that would last for decades. Babe Ruth's influence extended beyond the baseball diamond. He rose to prominence in American popular culture as a larger-than-life personality. His charm, joyous nature, and indisputable ability made him a revered figure at a time when the country was rebuilding from World War I and facing the rigors of the Great Depression. T

hroughout his career, Babe Ruth not only changed baseball but also broke through racial boundaries. In 1920, he played an exhibition game against a team of Negro League All-Stars, defying the era's segregated customs and expressing his conviction in equality. Off the field, Babe Ruth's demeanor matched his status as a sports star. He was well-known for his philanthropy and commitment to charitable activities. He went to children's hospitals, raised money for numerous charities, and utilized his celebrity to make a difference in society. Babe Ruth's extraordinary journey culminated in 1935, when he announced his retirement from professional baseball.

At the time, his multiple records, including his incredible career home run total of 714, appeared untouchable. He had become a symbol of optimism, perseverance, and the American ideal, as well as the best baseball player of his period. Babe Ruth's retirement years, however, were not without difficulties. He struggled with health concerns, notably throat cancer, which took his life on August 16, 1948, at the age of 53.

The country lamented the passing of a great icon, but Babe Ruth's legacy lived on. Babe Ruth's imprint on baseball and American society has remained everlasting in the decades since his death. His name is linked with brilliance, and his records, while later broken, are still acknowledged as landmarks in the game's history. The force of persistence and drive is perhaps the greatest enduring lesson we can take from Babe Ruth's life. He climbed from a terrible life and a difficult environment to become one of the most renowned individuals in sports history. His love of baseball, along with his unwavering dedication, elevated him from a troubled adolescent to a national hero. Babe Ruth's tale shows us that no matter what our circumstances are, we can overcome hardship and achieve greatness with perseverance and a firm confidence in our ambitions.

Furthermore, Babe Ruth's charity efforts and willingness to use his celebrity for the benefit of others highlight the value of giving back to one's community and making a beneficial influence on society.

What did we take away from him?

Finally, Babe Ruth's path from a rough upbringing to baseball celebrity, as well as his long legacy as a symbol of perseverance, optimism, and charity, continue to inspire others to pursue their aspirations, overcome obstacles, and use their success for the greater good. His narrative exemplifies the transformational power of enthusiasm, hard effort, and unshakable faith in the potential of a brighter future. Babe Ruth will be remembered not simply as a baseball hero, but also as an American icon whose legacy will live on in the hearts of future generations.

"The way a team plays as a whole determines its success. You may have the greatest bunch of individual stars in the world, but if they don't play together, the club won't be worth a dime."

3

USAIN BOLT

"Worrying gets you nowhere. If you turn up worrying about how you're going to perform, you've already lost. Train hard, turn up, run your best, and the rest will take care of itself."

U sain Bolt, commonly recognized as the world's fastest man, is best renowned for his exceptional sprinting abilities and unrivaled supremacy in track and field. Bolt, who was born in Jamaica in 1986, exploded into the international stage with his incredible speed and personality. He holds the world records for both the 100 and 200 meters, demonstrating his exceptional sprinting talents.

Bolt's famous lightning bolt posture became a symbol of his amazing speed and enthusiastic demeanor. He accomplished the unique achievement of winning gold medals in three consecutive Olympic Games (2008, 2012, and 2016) in the 100 meters, 200 meters, and 4x100 meters relay.

Bolt's contagious charm and sportsmanship endeared him to admirers all around the world, in addition to his athletic exploits. He continues to be an example to young athletes, demonstrating that excellence can be attained with devotion, hard effort, and a joyous attitude to one's vocation. Bolt's effect on the global stage and legacy in athletics are everlasting, establishing his place as a great sporting icon.

The Lightning Bolt: Usain Bolt's Quest for Eternity

On August 21, 1986, a legend was born in the little hamlet of Sherwood Content, tucked among Jamaica's stunning scenery. Usain St. Leo Bolt was his name, and little did the world know that this lanky youngster would grow up to be the fastest man alive and one of history's most recognized sportsmen.

Usain Bolt's journey is one of remarkable skill, unshakable dedication, and an indomitable spirit. It's the story of how a little child from rural Jamaica rose from poor beginnings to become the "Lightning Bolt" who destroyed world records, electrified stadiums, and captured the hearts of millions.

Usain's upbringing in Sherwood Content was far from wealthy. Jennifer and Wellesley Bolt, his parents, worked hard to provide for their family. His father was a grocery shop owner, while his mother was a clerk. Although the family's resources were minimal, their love and support for Usain was unending.Usain shown an early aptitude for athletics as a toddler, and his exceptional speed was noticeable. He enjoyed playing cricket and soccer with his buddies, but it was on the track that he revealed his true talent. His cricket coach advised him to attempt running after observing his lightning pace.

Usain began competing in sprinting events in Waldensia Primary School, showcasing his natural potential. He was a tall, wiry lad with a notably longer stride than his opponents. Something unique was clearly building in the young Jamaican's legs.When he transferred to William Knibb Memorial High School, his potential shone even more. Usain began to refine his sprinting abilities under the tutelage of coach Pablo McNeil. He raced in a variety of track and field events, but the 200 meters and 400 meters piqued his interest.

Usain Bolt's first taste of international glory came in 2002, when he competed in the World Junior Championships in Kingston, Jamaica. He won the 200-meter event at the age of 15, breaking a world junior record. It was a foreshadowing of what was to come, a peek of the world-beater he would become.

Despite his early success, Usain encountered setbacks. Injuries and the demands of elite-level sport put his willpower to the strain. But it was in the face of hardship that his spirit and resolve shined the clearest. He refused to be deterred by setbacks and continued to pursue his aim of being the world's fastest man.Bolt made his Olympic debut in Athens, Greece, in 2004 at the age of 17. While he did not win a medal in that tournament, he did gain vital experience. It spurred his desire for achievement, and he returned to Jamaica with newfound zeal.

Usain Bolt's career was transformed in 2008 in the Beijing Olympics. He dominated the 100-meter and 200-meter events in a remarkable show of speed and power, shattering world records and winning gold medals in each. His triumphant gesture, arms spread like lightning bolts, became an iconic image of his might.His contagious charm and joyous attitude attracted him to the globe, not simply his athletic skill. Usain Bolt's post-race antics, which included dancing and posing for the audience, cemented his reputation both on and off the track. He reminded us that athletics may provide us joy and enjoyment.

Usain Bolt's success continued at the 2012 London Olympics, as he defended his 100-meter and 200-meter crowns. He became the first guy in Olympic history to win gold medals in both events back-to-back. His world records in both sprints remained unbroken, and he cemented his place in track and field history.

Usain Bolt had hurdles in the years that followed, including injuries and the rise of new opponents. His passion for the sport, as well as his persistent devotion to training and competition, kept him in the limelight.His Olympic career concluded in the 2016 Rio Olympics. Despite facing great opposition, he won the 100 meters, 200 meters, and 4x100 meters relay once more. He pulled off a historic "triple-triple," winning gold medals in all three events at three consecutive Olympics.

Usain Bolt's influence stretched much beyond the track. He utilized his celebrity and achievements to motivate future generations of Jamaican athletes and to support sports development in his own country. He founded the Usain Bolt Foundation to provide possibilities for Jamaican children and youth via education and sports.

He announced his retirement from competitive track and field in August 2017, following the World Championships in London. It was the end of an era, but his legacy would live on. His impact on the sport was indisputable, as was his standing as a global sports star.

Usain Bolt's path from a tiny hamlet in Jamaica to the peak of Olympic success reminded us of the strength of drive, passion, and self-belief throughout his career. His unwavering pursuit of perfection, effervescent personality, and unlimited charm won him followers all over the world. He demonstrated that hard effort and a passion for what you do can lead to great results.

Usain Bolt's tale demonstrates that greatness can emerge from the most unexpected places, that aspirations can become reality, and that even the fastest man on the planet can be anchored in humility and thankfulness. His legacy will live on as a source of inspiration for young sportsmen and dreamers throughout the world.

What can Usain Bolt teach us?

Finally, the story of Usain Bolt, Jamaica's Lightning Bolt, serves as a compelling reminder that the human spirit knows no limitations. Usain Bolt's life is a tribute to the boundless potential inside all of us, from his modest origins in Sherwood Content to his electric exploits on the international stage. He is more than simply a sprinter; he is a symbol of the unwavering determination to pursue one's aspirations and aim for the stars.

"Dreams are free. Goals have a cost. While you can daydream for free, goals don't come without a price. Time, effort, sacrifice, and sweat. How will you pay for your goals?"

4

SERENA WILLIAMS

"I really think a champion is defined not by their wins but by how they can recover when they fall."

Serena Williams is well-known for her supremacy in women's tennis, having won several Grand Slam titles as well as Olympic gold medals. Her strong serve, athleticism, and unwavering dedication have helped her establish herself as one of the best tennis players of all time. Serena is a forerunner for gender equality in sports, fighting for equal remuneration for female athletes aside from her on-court abilities. She is also well-known for her humanitarian endeavors and dedication to social justice causes, having used her platform to highlight topics such as racial inequity and police brutality. Serena's impact extends beyond tennis, as she continues to inspire people via her extraordinary accomplishments and activism for a more fair society.

From Compton to Court Dominance: Serena Williams' Willpower Triumph:

A little girl called Serena Jameka Williams was exposed to a sport that would change her life forever in the sun-drenched neighborhoods of Compton, California, where the sounds of hip-hop frequently drowned out the echoes of tennis balls. Serena Williams was born on September 26, 1981, and went on to become one of the greatest tennis players of all time, changing the sport and inspiring millions with her relentless dedication and indomitable spirit.

Serena's childhood was characterised by poor beginnings. Her parents, Richard Williams and Oracene Price, saw talent in their two daughters, Serena and Venus, from an early age. Despite their low resources, the Williams family was determined to provide their children opportunities for success. Richard Williams, who had no prior tennis knowledge, decided to train his daughters himself. He studied instructional videos and books, and he began to mold Serena's extraordinary gift with makeshift tennis courts and unwavering commitment. He envisioned a future in which his daughters would rule the tennis world, an outrageous idea at the time. Serena experienced not just the difficulties of mastering a demanding sport as a youngster, but also the terrible reality of Compton's neighborhoods. She practiced on courts where gunshots occasionally rang in the distance, a far cry from the manicured tennis clubs of her future.

Adversity, on the other hand, only spurred Serena's resolve to achieve. Later, she reflected on those early days, adding, "I never let anybody or anything get in the way of me and my dreams." Serena's competitive nature was obvious from the outset. She and Venus moved fast through the junior tennis levels, and their rise was spectacular. Serena became professional at the age of 14 in 1995, raising eyebrows but demonstrating her unwavering confidence. She has been noted for her unrivaled agility, strong serve, and unwavering work ethic throughout her career. She plays with a combination of aggressiveness and accuracy, making her a deadly opponent on any surface. Her incredible singles career has seen her win many Grand Slam championships, Olympic gold medals, and twice accomplish the coveted Serena Slam (holding all four Grand Slam titles at the same time).

Serena's most renowned achievement was winning her maiden Grand Slam championship at the US Open in 1999. She won the youngest Grand Slam singles champion in more than a decade at the age of 17. This triumph was a watershed moment not just for Serena, but also for women of color in professional tennis, as it broke down racial boundaries and opened the door for more diversity in the sport. Serena's success went beyond her own accomplishments. Her doubles combination with her sister Venus was similarly powerful, resulting to multiple victories and confirming their place as one of tennis' best doubles couples. T

he Williams sisters' tennis devotion and family relationship influenced a generation of tennis players. Serena Williams has experienced various hurdles throughout the years, including injuries, personal losses, and intense competition. Her capacity to overcome hardship demonstrates her mental toughness and perseverance. She has frequently commented, "I've had to learn to fight all my life - now I have to learn to smile." Things will work out if you smile." Serena endured one of her most important hurdles when she gave birth to her daughter, Alexis Olympia Ohanian Jr.,

in 2017. Motherhood added a new depth to her already extraordinary adventure. After a tough delivery, she suffered a series of operations but maintained the same tenacity and enthusiasm she shown on the tennis court. Serena Williams' comeback to professional tennis after having a child was nothing short of inspirational. She reached the Wimbledon final in 2018 and the US Open final in 2019, demonstrating her ability to reconcile parenthood with a high-level career. Serena Williams' influence extends beyond her sporting accomplishments. She is a trailblazer in sports for gender equality, fighting for equal remuneration for female athletes and challenging the existing quo. She has been a vocal supporter of racial justice, using her position to confront issues of injustice and prejudice. Serena Williams is a successful entrepreneur, fashion designer, and philanthropist off the court. She owns her own clothing brand and has invested in other enterprises. Her charitable contributions include the Serena Williams Fund, which supports educational and community-building activities.

What can we learn from Serena?

Serena Williams' incredible journey from Compton to tennis domination is a stunning monument to the human spirit's ability to persevere, persevere, and achieve. Her narrative is about more than simply tennis; it's about breaking down boundaries, defying obstacles, and motivating future generations to follow their ambitions. Serena's story teaches us that success is characterized by our unshakable devotion to our objectives and our courage to overcome hardship, not by where we come from or the hurdles we confront. Her legacy will live on in the annals of tennis history, but it also transcends sports, reminding us that we can achieve greatness in all facets of life if we have the heart of a champion. Serena Williams is more than a tennis player; she is an inspiration, a role model, and a symbol of the endless possibilities that await those who dare to dream and work relentlessly. to turn those dreams into reality.

"You have to believe in yourself when no one else does. That's what makes you a winner."

5

MUHAMMAD ALI

"Float like a butterfly, sting like a bee."

Muhammad Ali is most recognized for his diverse legacy outside of athletics. He is remembered as a boxing icon for his unrivaled talents in the ring, which won him the title of one of the best fighters in history. His spectacular footwork, lightning-fast punches, and charm within the boxing ring catapulted him to international stardom. His legacy, however, stretches far beyond boxing gloves and championship belts. He is admired for his bravery and conviction, most notably his refusal to be inducted into the Vietnam War on religious and moral reasons. This audacious attitude lost him his boxing titles and momentarily shelved his career, but it elevated him to international status as a symbol of resistance and conscientious objection.Ali's vocal support for civil rights and racial equality solidified his place as a cultural and social hero. He utilized his celebrity to further the cause of justice, becoming a pivotal figure in the civil rights movement.

Aside from activism, Muhammad Ali was involved in considerable humanitarian activity, displaying his dedication to make a good difference in society. He supported a variety of charity causes, generated funding for humanitarian projects, and advocated global peace and understanding.

Muhammad Ali: The All-Time Greatest

On January 17, 1942, in the heart of Louisville, Kentucky, a legend was born. He was born Cassius Marcellus Clay Jr., but the world knew him as Muhammad Ali, the self-proclaimed "Greatest of All Time." Ali's life is nothing short of remarkable, from his early years in segregated America to his incredible boxing career and his continuing Courage and Conviction Leave a Legacy.

Louisville as a child

Cassius Clay Jr. encountered the harsh realities of injustice and inequity as a child growing up in a racially segregated America. Cassius Clay Sr. painted signs for a job, while his mother, Odessa Clay, worked as a housekeeper. Despite their limited resources, they taught in their son the principles of hard labor, perseverance, and self-respect.

Cassius Sr. took young Cassius to boxing when he was 12 years old with the hopes of teaching him how to protect oneself in a racially heated environment. Cassius swiftly improved his talents and began competing in amateur bouts under the tutelage of Joe Martin, a local police officer and boxing instructor.

Cassius' innate skill for the sport was obvious from the outset. He had lightning-fast reflexes, incredible footwork, and an insatiable will to win. He won a slew of amateur trophies, including two National Golden Gloves titles and a gold medal in the light heavyweight event in the 1960 Olympics in Rome.

Ascending the Pecking Order

Cassius Clay became professional after returning from the Olympics, accompanied by his mentor and trainer, Angelo Dundee. On October 29, 1960, in his hometown of Louisville, he made his professional debut and won a six-round decision. Clay's outgoing demeanor and unconventional fighting technique rapidly made him a media phenomenon.

Clay received a shot at Sonny Liston's world heavyweight belt in 1964. He came into the battle as a huge underdog, but he utilized his quickness, agility, and continuous trash talk to emotionally unsettle Liston. "I am the greatest," Clay famously declared before the bout, would become a defining statement of his career.

Cassius Clay challenged Sonny Liston on February 25, 1964, at Miami Beach, Florida, in a fight that would go down in history as one of the biggest upsets in sports. Clay, who was only 22 years old at the time, defeated Liston via technical knockout in the seventh round to win the world heavyweight champion.

Cassius Clay stated after the bout that he had converted to Islam and changed his name to Muhammad Ali. This choice was welcomed with both acclaim and criticism, but Ali stayed firm in his beliefs and convictions.

The Vietnam War and the Right to Refuse Service

Muhammad Ali, as the world heavyweight champion, became a powerful presence both within and outside of the boxing arena. His rejection to be recruited into the United States military during the Vietnam War in 1967, however, would become one of the most momentous and contentious decisions of his life.

Ali refused to serve because of religious concerns and his opposition to the war. "I ain't got no quarrel with them Viet Cong," he famously stated. This judgment resulted in his boxing ban, the loss of his titles, and a three-year legal fight.

Throughout his exile from the sport he adored, Ali continued to speak out against injustice and inequity. His uncompromising devotion to his ideals inspired many and brought attention to civil rights and anti-war causes.

Ali's conviction was overturned unanimously by the United States Supreme Court in 1971, recognizing his right to conscientious objection. In 1970, he returned to the boxing ring and began the difficult process of recovering his belts.

The Rumble in the Jungle and the Manila Thrilla

One of Muhammad Ali's most memorable events occurred in 1974, when he fought the formidable George Foreman in Kinshasa, Zaire (now the Democratic Republic of the Congo). Ali was once again considered an underdog, since Foreman was known for his tremendous punching power.

Ali used a technique he nicknamed the "rope-a-dope," in which he reclined against the ropes and let Foreman exhaust himself with blows. Ali stunned Foreman with a barrage of punches in the eighth round, achieving a historic victory. This match, dubbed the "Rumble in the Jungle," demonstrated Ali's strategic acumen as well as his ability to overcome apparently insurmountable odds.

In 1975, Ali met Joe Frazier in the "Thrilla in Manila," a fight that would go down in history as one of the greatest and most grueling. The bout lasted 14 rounds, with both competitors pushing themselves to the limit. Although Ali was victorious, the combat took its toll on both men.

Legacy of Courage and Conviction

Muhammad Ali's bravery stretched well beyond the boxing arena throughout his life and career. He was an outspoken supporter of civil rights, racial equality, and humanitarian causes. He utilized his celebrity and position to protest injustice, inequality, and war.

Ali received various medals and distinctions for his achievements to society, including the Presidential Medal of Freedom. He continued to inspire generations with his unshakeable self-confidence, devotion to his principles, and iconic statements like "Float like a butterfly, sting like a bee."

He was diagnosed with Parkinson's disease in 1984, a condition thought to be connected to his boxing career. Despite the disease's physical toll, he remained involved in public life and continued to make humanitarian donations.He died at the age of 74 on June 3, 2016. His memory endures as a symbol of tenacity, fortitude, and sticking up for what one believes in.

What did we learn from him?

To summarize, Muhammad Ali's life exemplifies the strength of conviction, endurance, and the fortitude to stand up for one's values. From a little child in Louisville to world heavyweight champion to global icon of civil rights and humanitarianism, his path has been nothing short of incredible. Ali's legacy continues to inspire people both inside and beyond the ring to believe in themselves, fight for justice, and strive for greatness. He is indeed "The Greatest of All Time."

"It's the repetition of affirmations that leads to belief. And once that belief becomes a deep conviction, things begin to happen."

6

PELE

"Success is no accident. It is hard work, perseverance, learning, studying, sacrifice, and most of all, love of what you are doing or learning to do."

P elé is best known for transforming the world of football. Edson Arantes do Nascimento, born in 1940 in Brazil, rose to become the sport's global ambassador and an emblem of greatness. Pelé's extraordinary brilliance and prolific goal-scoring abilities won him the distinction of best footballer of all time. He is the only player to have won three FIFA World Cups (1958, 1962, and 1970). On the field, his dazzling skills, remarkable athleticism, and agility set new standards for the sport. Pelé was respected for his sportsmanship, humility, and commitment to the beautiful game in addition to his playing abilities. His influence on the world of football has spanned generations, motivating many individuals and countries to take up the sport, creating solidarity, and promoting the spirit of competitiveness and joy that football epitomizes.

Pelé: A Football Legend's Journey

On October 23, 1940, a star was born in the tranquil village of Três Coraçes, Brazil. Little did the world realize that the youngster who emerged from these humble beginnings would go on to become the greatest footballer the world had ever seen. Pelé, Edson Arantes do Nascimento, would go on to inspire millions, elevate the sport of football, and exemplify the real essence of an athletic icon.

Childhood and Football Addiction

Pelé's upbringing was far from fortunate. Growing up in poverty, he used to play football with a homemade ball made of rags and socks knotted together. Sport became his passion and an escape from the difficulties of his early existence. He refined his talents by running barefoot through the streets of Bauru, a town he and his family moved to when he was a toddler.

Pelé joined the youth squad of Santos Futebol Clube at the age of 15, a move that would change the path of his life. His extraordinary potential was immediately recognized, and he made his professional debut with Santos at the age of 16. The world got its first sight of the youngster who would change football forever.

Ascend to International Notoriety

Pelé's rise to worldwide prominence was expedited at the 1958 FIFA World Cup in Sweden. He became the youngest player in World Cup history to score in the final at the age of 17. Pelé's brilliant skills, fast movement, and goal-scoring abilities led Brazil to its first World Cup title, and he finished the tournament as the tournament's leading scorer.

Pelé continued to dominate football on a worldwide scale, and the world watched in wonder. He was a key figure in Brazil's World Cup victories in 1962 and 1970, becoming the first player to win three FIFA World Cups. His influence on the sport was unrivaled, and he is still the only player to have accomplished this amazing achievement.

Pelé's game was distinguished by his extraordinary talents, flawless ball control, and incredible ability to score goals from any position on the pitch. He possessed a natural grasp of the game, a vision that enabled him to generate opportunities for his team-mates, and an unrivaled work ethic.

Triumphs and setbacks

Pelé's career was not without its hurdles, despite its splendor and success. Injuries threatened to derail his path at several stages, but his tenacity and devotion to his trade allowed him to recover time and time again.

Pelé's contributions to the sport extended beyond his on-field achievements. He was a global ambassador for football, helping to popularize the sport all over the world. His presence elevated football to new heights, capturing the attention of supporters of all ages and backgrounds.

Legacy and the Beautiful Game

Pelé's influence on football stretched beyond his outstanding individual performances. He personified the sport's beauty and grace, bringing it to the level of an art form. His goals were more than simply goals; they were magical moments that left onlookers speech-less. His humility, sportsmanship, and true passion for the game helped him become a popular character both on and off the field.

Pelé retired from professional football in 1977, leaving behind an unrivaled career. He has almost 1,000 goals in his career, an unrivaled number. His impact on the sport was enormous, and he became a global legend.

Pelé's post-retirement activities included humanitarian endeavors, advocacy for children's rights, and promotion of football as a tool for constructive social change. His humanitarian initiatives demonstrated his dedication to make the world a better place.

What can we take away from him?

We may learn the lasting worth of talent, hard effort, and persistent dedication from Pelé's incredible life and career. From poor origins to global football icon, his experience tells us that perseverance and commitment can conquer any obstacle. Pelé's humility, sportsmanship, and passion for the game teach us how important it is to stay grounded and appreciate what we do. His ability to inspire millions both on and off the field demonstrates the power of athletics to unite, empower, and offer joy to people all around the world. Pelé's legacy serves as a testament to the transformative power of sports and the indomitable spirit of those who pursue their dreams relentlessly.

"The more difficult the victory, the greater the happiness in winning."

7

KOBE BRYANT

"I'll do whatever it takes to win games, whether it's sitting on a bench waving a towel, handing a cup of water to a teammate, or hitting the game-winning shot."

Kobe Bryant is widely regarded as one of the best basketball players of all time. He is recognized for his remarkable scoring ability, tenacity, and competitive attitude. Kobe Bryant's two-decade NBA career with the Los Angeles Lakers produced five NBA titles, multiple All-Star berths, and countless scoring records. He was recognized for his clutch performances in crucial situations, giving him the moniker "The Black Mamba." Off the court, Kobe was a symbol of hard work and devotion to one's profession, pursuing greatness in a variety of activities such as filmmaking and storytelling. His influence extends beyond basketball, acting as an inspiration to players and others all throughout the world.

Basketball Origins and Childhood

Kobe Bryant was born into a basketball-loving household. Joe "Jellybean" Bryant, his father, was a former NBA player, and his maternal grandpa, Joe "Papa Joe" Bryant, was also a former NBA player. As a result, Kobe was exposed to basketball at a young age, and the sport rapidly became a big part of his life.The Bryant family's basketball connection brought them to Italy in 1984, when Kobe was just six years old. Joe Bryant played professionally in the Italian league in order to further his basketball career. Kobe began to build his love for the game in Italy, improving his talents and seeing other styles of play.

Childhood in Italy

Kobe's formative years in Italy were spent not only playing basketball but also learning about various cultures and languages. He swiftly adjusted to life in Europe, learning Italian and acquiring a global outlook that would later distinguish him from his contemporaries.

As Kobe grew and matured, his love for basketball grew stronger. He looked up to NBA players like Magic Johnson and Larry Bird, studied their games and aspired to be like them. He had no idea that his personal journey would lead him to the summit of the sport.

Return to the United States of America

The Bryants returned to the United States in 1991, residing in the Philadelphia suburbs. Kobe would go on to attend Lower Merion High School, where he would build a reputation for himself on the basketball court. Although his outstanding talent and hard ethic were obviously apparent, he faced a unique set of hurdles.

Not only was Kobe the son of a former NBA player, but he was also the nephew of another former NBA player,

John "Chubby" Cox. Expectations weighed heavily on his youthful shoulders. People were interested in seeing if he could live up to his family's basketball history.

The High School Superstar

Kobe's time at Lower Merion High School would go down in history as legendary. In his senior year, he was a scoring machine, averaging 31.1 points, 10.4 rebounds, and 5.2 assists per game. His outstanding play won him the title of top high school basketball player in the country, and he was chosen to the McDonald's All-American Team.

Despite his high school accomplishments, Kobe had doubts about his ability to enter the NBA straight out of high school. The transition from high school to the professionals was uncommon at the time, and it was regarded as a dangerous choice. But Kobe was unfazed; he was confident in his ability and opted to enter the 1996 NBA Draft, a choice that would affect the rest of his life.

Early Challenges and the NBA Draft

The 1996 NBA Draft marked a watershed moment in Kobe's life. The Charlotte Hornets drafted him 13th overall, but his time with the Hornets was short. He was immediately transferred to the Los Angeles Lakers, a move that would forever associate his name with one of the NBA's most legendary clubs.

Kobe's debut season in the NBA had flashes of greatness as well as the difficulties that come with youth and inexperience. He struggled at times to find his position on a team that contained established talents such as Shaquille O'Neal and Eddie Jones. However, Kobe's ability and promise were evident, and with his electric dunks and daring style of play, he immediately became a fan favorite.

The Legendary Mentorship

Kobe Bryant was fortunate to play with a team that included seasoned players and mentors. Shaquille O'Neal, in particular, mentored the inexperienced newcomer. Shaq saw Kobe's potential and encouraged him to practice harder and improve his talents. The two's friendship would become a defining feature in the Lakers' early-2000s dominance.

Kobe's talent grew stronger with each passing year. His devotion to the game was unwavering, and he frequently spent hours polishing his talents after practice had ended. He studied video, worked extensively on his shot, and perfected his footwork.

Success in the NBA during the Shaq-Kobe Era

The Los Angeles Lakers had a golden age in the late 1990s and early 2000s, owing in large part to the dynamic tandem of Shaquille O'Neal and Kobe Bryant. From 2000 to 2002, the combination led the Lakers to three straight NBA championships, establishing themselves as one of the most powerful duos in basketball history.

During both championship campaigns, Kobe's development as a complete player was clear. He was a prolific striker as well as a fierce defender and playmaker. He became the NBA's youngest player to achieve 20,000 career points, demonstrating his scoring ability.

Controversies and Obstacles

Kobe's journey was not without difficulties and controversy. In 2003, he was accused of sexual assault in Colorado, which drew heavy media scrutiny and threatened to ruin his image. Although the legal actions were subsequently discontinued, the episode left a lasting impression on Kobe's public image.

Kobe was also dealing with internal friction inside the Lakers organization during this turbulent time. His relationship with Shaquille O'Neal deteriorated, and the Lakers' title streak ended with a loss in the 2004 NBA Finals.

The Mamba Mindset Spreads

The spirit of the Mamba Mentality began to take root in Kobe's life during these tough times. As he characterized it, the Mamba Mentality was one of persistent pursuit of excellence, unshakable self-belief, and an unflinching work ethic. Kobe saw setbacks and adversity as chances to grow and enhance his game.

Kobe continued to flourish as one of the league's top players in the seasons following the Lakers' championship run. He led the league in scoring, won NBA MVP honors, and was named to the All-Star team year after year.

The Redemption of Kobe vs. Boston in the 2008 NBA Finals

The stage was set for one of the most fierce and dramatic rivalries in NBA history. Kobe Bryant, the Black Mamba, stood in one corner, a determined competitor with a burning desire to add another title to his brilliant career. The Boston Celtics, a historic organization aching for revenge after a 22-year title drought, were in the opposite corner.

The Los Angeles Lakers, led by Kobe Bryant, faced the Boston Celtics, led by Kevin Garnett, Paul Pierce, and Ray Allen, in the 2008 NBA Finals. The rivalry was about more than simply two clubs; it was about legacy and pride. The Celtics were desperate to reclaim their championship glories, while Kobe wanted to prove that he could win without Shaquille O'Neal.

The series was a back-and-forth fight, with both sides demonstrating tenacity. Each game was a battle of wills between basketball heavyweights. The Celtics had a dominating 3-2 series lead, but Kobe and the Lakers refused to give up.

Game 6 of the series would go down in history as a watershed moment. Kobe, dressed in purple and gold for the Lakers, unleashed his scoring skills with a stunning 38-point effort. The Lakers scored a critical victory with their backs against the wall, requiring a Game 7 to be played.

As the series neared its conclusion, the suspense was evident. The Celtics won their 17th NBA title with a 131-92 victory in a low-scoring defensive duel. Kevin Garnett, who memorably exclaimed during the postgame celebration, "Anything is possible!" epitomized the Celtics' road of redemption.

While Kobe and the Lakers were defeated in 2008, their rivalry was cemented in basketball history. It exemplified competitors at the height of their sport's perseverance, enthusiasm, and pure resolve. Kobe's unwavering pursuit of excellence, as well as the Celtics' comeback tale, served as sources of motivation for both players and spectators.

In the years afterwards, Kobe has won two more NBA titles, cementing his position as one of the best players of all time. The intense and dramatic 2008 NBA Finals battle reminded us that even in defeat, the spirit of competitiveness and the quest of perfection can drive us to achieve higher heights. It served as a reminder that the actual soul of sports is found in the journey, rivalries, and the tenacious human spirit that pulls us ahead regardless of the outcome.

Kobe's Farewell: A Legendary Night

The Staples Center in Los Angeles was filled to the rafters on April 13, 2016. It was a night that would be remembered on calendars and in the hearts of Lakers fans all across the world. It was the night of Kobe Bryant's final game, a basketball legend's swan song.

Kobe had announced his retirement earlier in the season, and every game since has been a farewell tour, an opportunity for fans, peers, and opponents to pay their respects to a guy who had spent two decades of his life to the Los Angeles Lakers.

The energy inside the Staples Center was palpable. Fans wore Kobe shirts and held placards that said "Thank You, Kobe" and "Mamba Forever." It was a sea of purple and gold, a monument to one man's enduring influence on a city and a sport.

As the game began, it became clear that Kobe was not willing to merely play out his final minutes on the field. He was there to put on a show, to show the world why he was one of the best players of all time. The crowd erupted with enthusiasm and nostalgia with each shot he took and move he made.

That night, Kobe's performance was nothing short of legendary. He led all scorers with 60 points in their final game. It was a vintage Kobe effort, complete with clutch shots, fadeaways, and an unwavering will to win. With the Lakers down in the fourth quarter, Kobe went on a scoring rampage, willing his team to victory.

Kobe stood at the free-throw line with seconds remaining on the clock. The game was tied, and the significance of the moment hung in the balance. He hit both free shots with poise, giving the Lakers a lead they would not lose. As the last buzzer rang, the audience exploded in joy.

Kobe had not only delivered a victory, but also a performance for the ages. "Mamba out," he said to the throng, a fitting goodbye from the Black Mamba himself.

He said goodbye that night went beyond basketball. It was a monument to the force of determination, perseverance, and a real competitor's indomitable spirit. It served as a reminder that legends are formed over years of hard effort and a tireless pursuit of greatness.

As Kobe walked off the floor for the final time as a Laker, he left behind a legacy that will live on in sports history. He demonstrated that no desire is too huge, no struggle too difficult, and no moment too grand. Kobe Bryant's farewell game was more than just a farewell; it was an encouraging reminder that we can achieve the remarkable with passion, perseverance, and unshakable confidence.

On January 26, 2020, Kobe Bryant was killed in a helicopter crash. Kobe, his daughter Gianna, and seven others were aboard when the helicopter crashed into a hillside in Calabasas, California. The catastrophe claimed the lives of all nine people on board.

Kobe's untimely and sad death shocked the globe, since he was not just an iconic player in basketball but also a beloved and respected man. He was well-known for his great talent, work ethic, and passion to his sport, as well as his charity activities and position as a mentor to future athletes.

The sad tragedy was a tremendous loss not just for the basketball community, but also for individuals all across the world who respected Kobe's tenacity, leadership, and dedication to perfection. Kobe Bryant's legacy lives on, with his influence spreading well beyond the basketball floor. He will be regarded as a great legend and a source of inspiration for many.

What did we learn from Kobe Bryant?

For starters, his consistent work ethic demonstrates the strength of unrelenting determination and ongoing self-improvement. Kobe's long hours of practice and dedication to improving his talents remind us that greatness is earned through sacrifice.

Second, the Mamba Mentality, a word invented by Kobe himself, represents a fearless approach to problems. It teaches us to see hardship as a chance for progress, to never settle for mediocrity, and to have unflinching faith in ourselves.Kobe's tenacity is yet another vital lesson. His ability to bounce back from injuries, disputes, and defeats highlights the value of persistence and refusing to be defined by failure.His devotion to his art emphasizes the importance of discovering one's genuine passion and giving it one's best. Basketball was more than just a job for Kobe; it was a calling.

Kobe demanded perfection from himself and his colleagues as a leader, demonstrating the transforming potential of good leadership in accomplishing collective goals.His path from high school to the NBA and through many obstacles emphasizes the value of endurance and unflinching dedication to one's ambitions.Kobe's influence stretches well beyond athletics. His forays into filmmaking, storytelling, and philanthropy demonstrate that our influence may extend beyond our major interests, allowing us to make a constructive mark on society.

Finally, Kobe Bryant's life acts as a constant source of inspiration, reminding us that with dedication, perseverance, and the Mamba Mentality, we can overcome hurdles and strive for excellence in our lives. any endeavor.

"The most important thing is to try and inspire people so that they can be great in whatever they want to do."

8

MIA HAMM

"Celebrate what you've accomplished, but raise the bar a little higher each time you succeed."

F ew names in soccer carry as much weight as Mia
Hamm's. Her path from a little girl with a passion

for soccer to one of the greatest soccer players of all time is one of devotion, resilience, and the unflinching pursuit of perfection. But Mia's influence extends far beyond the soccer field; she has left an indelible stamp on the sport and served as an inspiration to future generations.

Early Childhood and Family Influence

Mia Hamm grew raised in a close-knit family that loved athletics. She was born Mariel Margaret Hamm on March 17, 1972, in Selma, Alabama. Bill Hamm, her father, was an Air Force pilot, and Stephanie Hamm worked as a secretary. Mia was the youngest of six children, and her siblings were instrumental in instilling in her a passion of soccer.

Mia relocated to Wichita Falls, Texas, with her family when she was a child. Her older brother, Garrett, introduced her to soccer here. The Hamm brothers spent endless hours developing their abilities and cultivating a passion for the beautiful game in their garden.

Beginnings That Are Difficult

Despite her early love of soccer, Mia experienced gender-related obstacles as she desired to play at the highest level. females' soccer was not as popular or funded at the time as boys' soccer, therefore there were less possibilities for females to engage in organized leagues. Undaunted, Mia and her parents looked for possibilities for her to further her education.

Mia's drive and aptitude were instantly apparent as she succeeded in local and state-level tournaments. Even at such a young age, her speed, agility, and scoring ability were unrivaled. This youthful prodigy caught the attention of the soccer world.

Stardom in High School

Mia's outstanding soccer abilities won her a scholarship to the University of North Carolina (UNC). However, prior to attending UNC, she excelled at Notre Dame Catholic High School in Wichita Falls. During her four years there, she set a national high school record by scoring 158 goals in four years.

Mia represented the United States in international events as a teenager, becoming one of the youngest players to secure a berth on the U.S. Women's National Team.

At UNC, dominance

Mia Hamm's stay at the University of North Carolina was a watershed moment in her soccer career. She not only improved her talents under the tutelage of famed coach Anson Dorrance, but she also made lifelong connections and a winning mindset that would influence her career.

Mia led the University of North Carolina to four straight NCAA national titles from 1989 to 1993. She was a three-time All-American who received multiple individual honors. On the field, her exceptional scoring ability, speed, and technical proficiency made her a force to be reckoned with.

A World Cup winner

Mia Hamm's meteoric ascent did not stop at the college level. She was instrumental in the United States Women's National Team's international success. When the United States team won the FIFA Women's World Cup in 1991, she was the youngest player to do so at the age of 19.

Mia's contributions to women's soccer extended beyond her outstanding abilities. She became a symbol of the sport's popularity and expansion, encouraging a new generation of female soccer players.

Olympic Gold and Long-Term Success

Mia Hamm has continued to flourish on the international level. She was a vital member of the

United States Women's National Team that won gold at the 1996 Atlanta Olympics, the first to feature women's soccer. Her ability to lead and score goals made her a popular figure in the soccer world.

Mia's career may have peaked at the 1999 FIFA Women's World Cup. She helped lead the United States team to victory as the tournament's best scorer, captivating the hearts of fans across the country. The final, which the United States won in spectacular fashion against China, is still one of the most viewed soccer games in United States history.

A Legacy That Extends Beyond Soccer

Mia Hamm's influence went well beyond the soccer field. She utilized her position to push for gender equality in sports and was a driving force behind Title IX, a federal statute that outlaws gender discrimination in education and athletics.

Mia was a dedicated humanitarian off the field. She founded the Mia Hamm Foundation to raise finances and awareness for families in need, particularly those affected by bone marrow illnesses.

Legacy and Retirement

Mia Hamm announced her retirement from professional soccer in 2004. With 158 international goals, she held the record for the most international goals scored by any soccer player, male or female, at the time of her retirement.

Mia Hamm's legacy lives on not just via her achievements and awards, but also through her influence on the global expansion of women's soccer. She motivated other young girls to pursue their athletic aspirations and broke down barriers for women in sports. Her influence extended beyond the soccer pitch, making her a global icon and a source of inspiration.

What can Mia Hamm teach us?

Her unwavering pursuit of soccer brilliance illustrates the benefits of hard effort and determination. Mia's influence extends beyond athletics, teaching us the value of using our platform to advocate for gender equality and philanthropic causes. She motivates us to overcome obstacles, push for change, and leave a lasting legacy that transcends our accomplishments. Mia Hamm's life demonstrates that greatness lies not only in personal success but also in making a positive impact on society, especially in empowering future generations of athletes and advocates for equality.ation for athletes and non-athletes alike.

"The vision of a champion is someone who is drenched in sweat at the point of exhaustion when no one else is watching."

9

KHABIB NURMAGOMEDOV

"Fighting is not about showing how tough you are or how big your ego is. It's about respect and being a martial artist."

K habib Nurmagomedov is a well-known MMA fighter with a 29-0 record that demonstrates his remarkable wrestling abilities and ground-and-pound style. He's become a symbol of authority and supremacy in the sport, giving him the moniker "The Eagle." His ground-and-pound technique is impressive, with accurate and forceful attacks. Khabib's flexibility as a submission artist also demonstrates his skill. His time as UFC Lightweight Champion was a pinnacle achievement, with each defense demonstrating his undying dedication to brilliance. Khabib became a cultural superstar in Dagestan and Russia outside of the cage, garnering him thousands of admirers worldwide. His MMA history is a monument to the strength of dedication, discipline, and an unwavering drive to succeed. Khabib Nurmagomedov will be regarded as a real sporting great, a symbol of perfection, and an inspiration to fighters and fans alike.

Khabib Nurmagomedov: The Soaring Spirit of the Eagle

On September 20, 1988, a little child called Khabib Nurmagomedov was born amid the rocky and unforgiving landscape of Dagestan, a territory situated in Russia's Caucasus Mountains. The world had no idea that this simple boy would one day become a symbol of extraordinary strength, steadfast perseverance, and profound humility. Khabib's journey from the Dagestan highlands to the summit of mixed martial arts (MMA) is proof of the indestructible human spirit.

Khabib was born into a family with a long history of involvement in combat sports. His father, Abdulmanap Nurmagomedov, was an accomplished wrestler and respected instructor, and his younger brother, Abubakar, would also pursue an MMA career. Khabib was involved in the world of martial arts from an early age, studying the foundations of wrestling and grappling under the careful supervision of his father.

Dagestan, a place known for its harsh terrain and resilient history, instilled in Khabib a tough determination that would serve him well in the years to come. His upbringing's adversity only spurred his tireless quest of excellence.Khabib's path to becoming a world-class fighter began with his love of wrestling. He polished his abilities via long hours of practice, sometimes suffering difficult exercises in harsh conditions. His father's guidance was crucial in his growth, emphasizing discipline, hard effort, and an unyielding dedication to his trade.

Khabib made his professional MMA debut in 2008, and it was quickly evident that he has exceptional potential. In the cage, his distinctive grappling technique of relentless takedowns and stifling ground control became his hallmark. Khabib got the moniker "The Eagle" for his supremacy and the glory he gave to his motherland as he won in many competitions, including the UFC.

Khabib's ascension in the UFC, the world's best MMA organization, was meteoric. With each encounter, he demonstrated his unrivaled wrestling prowess and unbreakable spirit. In 2018, he competed for the UFC Lightweight Championship against Al Iaquinta. Khabib put up a strong performance to win the championship and cement his place as one of the top fighters in the world.

What transpired after the bout, though, would define Khabib's career. Overwhelmed by victory, he stormed out of the cage and into the audience, igniting a melee with Conor McGregor's side. Khabib eventually apologized for his conduct, displaying uncommon humility and self-awareness in the middle of victory.

In July 2020, Khabib's father and coach, Abdulmanap Nurmagomedov, died as a result of COVID-19 problems. Abdulmanap was a revered figure in the MMA world as well as Khabib's mentor. His death had a great effect on Khabib, who resolved to carry on his father's legacy by competing at the highest level.

Khabib's most memorable moment occurred in October 2020, when he faced Justin Gaethje in UFC 254. The battle was very special since it was his first fight since his father died. Despite the emotional weight on his shoulders, Khabib executed a magnificent performance, submitting Gaethje in the second round to retain his lightweight championship.

What happened next was a touching and emotional scene. Khabib collapsed on his knees in the octagon's middle, struck by anguish and the weight of his father's absence. He declared his retirement from MMA in a poignant post-fight interview, promising his mother that he would never longer fight without his father at his side.

Khabib Nurmagomedov's Biggest Fight: An Epic Duel

In the world of MMA, one fight stood out as the apex of Khabib Nurmagomedov's career—a battle that would put his mettle to the test like never before. It was a collision of titans, a confrontation between him and his most ferocious foe, Conor McGregor. This was a clash of styles, egos, and legacies, not just a battle.

The anticipation for this match was palpable. McGregor, famed for his brazen charm and striking power, was the UFC Lightweight Champion who had won the hearts of fans all over the world. Khabib, on the other side, was the stoic and dominating champion with an unblemished record and a wrestling pedigree unequaled.

The world watched in wonder as the two warriors entered the octagon on that fateful night. The tension was tangible, and the stakes were higher than ever before. It was not just a fight for the title belt for Khabib, but also a battle to prove that his wrestling superiority could beat McGregor's striking genius.

The opening round showcased McGregor's striking abilities. He landed strikes and came dangerously near to submitting Khabib. But Khabib's unshakeable heart and desire shined through. He stayed calm in the face of the storm and kept to his game plan.

His grappling prowess began to take control as the battle proceeded. He completed takedowns with accuracy, using his wrestling prowess to keep McGregor on the ground. Khabib doggedly chased victory, demonstrating extraordinary coolness in the face of adversity round every round.

It happened in the fourth round. Khabib won via submission, forcing McGregor to tap out. The arena roared, but what followed was a real sportsmanship demonstration. Rather of gloating in his triumph, Khabib showed respect for both his opponent and the sport itself.

This game was about more than just capturing a title or resolving a feud. It exemplified the qualities that constitute a champion: devotion, discipline, and a never-ending quest of greatness. The triumph of Khabib Nurmagomedov against Conor McGregor inspired ambitious warriors and dreamers all around the world.

It showed us that no matter what the odds are, we can conquer any difficulty with unflinching determination and a champion's attitude. Khabib's triumph demonstrated that, in the face of hardship, one can rise above it and emerge stronger than before.

Khabib Nurmagomedov's biggest fight was more than simply a victory in the octagon; it was a triumph of the human spirit. It demonstrated that champions are defined not just by their ability but also by their character. Khabib's legacy will eternally inspire us to follow our ambitions with unflinching drive, to conquer hurdles, and to stand strong in the face of adversity, because genuine greatness is about how we conduct ourselves on the path, not simply how we win.

His legacy extends beyond his unrivaled octagon success. He is admired not only for his fighting abilities, but also for his humility, respect for his opponents, and devotion to his family and faith. His unshakable dedication to honoring his father's lessons demonstrates the principles ingrained in him at an early age.

Khabib's tale touches people all across the world, not just as a champion, but also as a symbol of perseverance, humility, and the everlasting human spirit. He continues to be an inspiration to young fighters, sportsmen, and others experiencing difficulties. His legacy teaches us that greatness is characterized not just by achievements, but also by one's character, humility, and grace in both triumph and tragedy.

Khabib Nurmagomedov's retirement was declared official after he resigned the UFC lightweight championship in March 2021. He retired as an unbeaten champion with a 29-0 record, confirming his place as one of the best fighters in MMA history.

What can we take away from him?

We may learn the characteristics of steadfast determination, unrivaled work ethic, and the necessity of honouring one's heritage from Khabib Nurmagomedov. His unbeaten career exemplifies the strength of perseverance and the unwavering pursuit of perfection. Khabib's humility and sportsmanship in both triumph and defeat show us the importance of respecting opponents and protecting the sport's integrity. His willingness to put family first and keep promises illustrates the importance of values and beliefs over personal glory. The legacy of Khabib Nurmagomedov teaches us that genuine greatness is defined not only by accomplishments but also by character and ideals.

10

TOM BRADY

"When you have something to prove, there's nothing greater than a challenge."

Tom Brady is widely regarded as one of the best quarterbacks in NFL history. Seven Super Bowl titles, an NFL record, and five Super Bowl Most Valuable Player (MVP) honors characterize his career. He is known for his unrivaled ability to lead teams to victory, his high football IQ, and his legendary clutch exploits. Brady is known as the "GOAT" (Greatest of All Time) for his longevity, constantly competing at an elite level well into his 40s. His vision, work ethic, and dedication to greatness have raised the bar for success in the world of professional football.

Tom Brady's Story of Valour and Glory

Few names in American sports history are as well-known as Tom Brady's. His climb from an unknown sixth-round draft pick to seven-time Super Bowl champion is a testament to skill, persistence, and a never-ending quest of excellence. Tom Brady's story, on the other hand, is one of determination, leadership, and the never-ending pursuit of perfection.

On August 3, 1977, Thomas Edward Patrick Brady Jr. was born in San Mateo, California. He was born with a strong competitive streak and a passion for sports. Tom Brady Sr., his father, instilled in him the virtues of hard work, dedication, and achieving one's ambitions.

Brady was a standout in high school football and baseball. He chose to join the University of Michigan despite garnering minimal interest from NCAA football clubs. Brady had significant competition for the starting quarterback position during his junior year, but he eventually won it.

Brady's football intelligence and leadership talents emerged at Michigan. He led the Wolverines to the 2000 Orange Bowl victory, capping off an outstanding collegiate career.

Tom Brady's life was changed forever by the NFL Draft in 2000. The New England Patriots selected him in the sixth round, as the 199th overall pick—an incident that would go down in NFL history. Brady's decision was influenced by concerns about his athleticism and prospects as a pro quarterback.

Brady joined the Patriots as the seasoned Drew Bledsoe's backup quarterback. However, Bledsoe's injury early in the 2001 season prompted Brady to take over as starter. What occurred next was the beginning of an unbelievable adventure.

Under Tom Brady's guidance, the New England Patriots embarked on a dynasty that would redefine success in the NFL. Brady's meticulous preparation, football intellect, and clutch performances contributed to the Patriots winning three Super Bowls in four years (2001, 2003, and 2004).

His working relationship with Bill Belichick was marked by a desire to win, attention to detail, and a never-ending drive to improve. They worked together to create a winning culture that valued team performance over individual accolades.

The discussion regarding Brady's place in NFL history intensified significantly as his career continued. He was widely likened to Hall of Famers Joe Montana and Johnny Unitas. Brady's ability to perform at a high level far into his 30s and 40s further fueled the flames.

In Super Bowl LI, Brady orchestrated one of the greatest comebacks in NFL history, overcoming a 28-3 deficit to win his sixth championship. The triumph confirmed his status as one of the all-time great quarterbacks, and the acronym "GOAT" (Greatest of All Time) became synonymous with his name.

After 20 seasons with the Patriots, Brady shocked the sports world by signing with the Tampa Bay Buccaneers in 2020. The move signaled the start of a new chapter in his great career, as well as an opportunity to demonstrate himself outside of the Patriots' system.

Brady led the Buccaneers to Super Bowl LV victory in his first season, earning his sixth championship ring at the age of 43. His ability to adapt to a new group and prosper in a strange environment added to his renown.

Tom Brady's impact goes beyond football. He is well-known for his team leadership, work ethic, and devotion. His persistent pursuit of perfection serves as a model for both aspiring athletes and professionals.

Brady commits his off-field time to charities and charitable causes. He established the TB12 Foundation to help young athletes and promote health and fitness. His advocacy for a holistic approach to training and well-being has impacted many others.

Throughout his career, Tom Brady has faced several setbacks and difficulties. Despite being a late-round draft pick and dealing with injuries and criticism, his ability to bounce back and excel in adversity is a testament to his mental strength and persistence.

Tom Brady's incredible journey from sixth-round draft pick to seven-time Super Bowl champion is nothing short of remarkable. His persistent pursuit of greatness, flexibility, leadership, and humanitarian actions make him a role model both on and off the field.

What can we take away from Him?

Tom Brady's path teaches important life lessons. His meteoric climb from late-round NFL draft pick to seven-time Super Bowl winner exemplifies the power of determination and tenacity. Brady's dedication to self-improvement and adaptation emphasizes the significance of constant growth and learning.

On and off the field, his leadership characteristics serve as an example for aspiring leaders. His ability to motivate and unite colleagues, along with his unwavering work ethic, has been critical to his success.

Brady's mental fortitude in high-pressure situations highlights the need of being calm in stressful situations, which is useful in many parts of life.

Brady's devotion to charity and giving back, in addition to his on-field triumphs, emphasizes the value of leveraging success as a platform for constructive change.

In summary, Tom Brady's journey tells us that genuine greatness is achieved through perseverance, flexibility, leadership, and an unflinching dedication to personal development. His story provides as motivation for others aspiring to greatness. in any field.

"I think the mental toughness of a football team and the resolve is way more important than any physical skill that you have."

11

WAYNE GRETZKY

"The highest compliment that you can pay me is to say that I work hard every day, that I never dog it." This quote underscores the value of consistent effort and work ethic in achieving success.

Wayne Gretzky is widely regarded as the most prolific scorer in National Hockey League (NHL) history. He is well-known for his unrivaled ability to read the game, anticipate plays, and generate scoring chances for himself and his teammates. Gretzky has multiple NHL records, including the most career goals, assists, and points, establishing him as the all-time top scorer. His leadership, modesty, and commitment to team success were legendary, gaining him the respect of both spectators and players. Gretzky's influence on the sport stretched beyond the rink, as he helped promote hockey in non-traditional areas, leaving an indelible impression on the sports world.

Wayne Gretzky: The Journey of the Great One

In the realm of hockey, no name stands out more than Wayne Gretzky's. His path from a little village in Canada to becoming a sports hero is nothing short of miraculous. He is widely recognized as the best player to ever grace the rink. Wayne Gretzky's narrative, known simply as "The Great One," is a monument to brilliance, hard effort, and an unshakable love for the game.

Wayne Douglas Gretzky was born in Brantford, Ontario, Canada on January 26, 1961. His passion for hockey was clear from a young age. Walter Gretzky, Wayne's father, created a backyard rink for Wayne and his siblings, where Wayne's remarkable talents would blossom.

Wayne had an extraordinary ability to read the game even as a toddler. He possessed an uncanny ability to predict where the puck would be, which put him apart from his contemporaries. Wayne's progress as a footballer was aided by his father's coaching and encouragement.

Wayne Gretzky's abilities became more apparent as he went through the levels of minor hockey. At the age of 16, he joined the Sault Ste. Marie Greyhounds of the

Ontario Hockey League (OHL) and made an immediate impression. In his debut season, he set a league record by scoring 70 goals and amassing 182 points.

During his stint in the OHL, Wayne gained the moniker "The Great One." His domination on the ice was unrivaled, as was his ability to read the game, predict plays, and set up teammates.

Wayne Gretzky made the transition to professional hockey in 1978, signing with the Indianapolis Racers of the World Hockey Association (WHA). However, his time there was brief since the squad was experiencing financial troubles. Gretzky was quickly moved to the Edmonton Oilers, altering the trajectory of his career and the history of the NHL.

The arrival of Wayne Gretzky in Edmonton coincided with the team's admission into the NHL. It signaled the start of a period of dominance for both Gretzky and the Oilers. His contributions to the squad were immediate, as he led the league in scoring and won the first of many Hart Trophies as the NHL's Most Valuable Player.

The Oilers, headed by Gretzky, dominated the NHL during the 1980s. They won four Stanley Cups in five years, with Gretzky continuously smashing records and achieving new levels of greatness. His ability to improve others around him was a defining feature of his game, as he picked up assists and goals at an alarming rate.

When Wayne Gretzky was moved to the Los Angeles Kings in 1988, the hockey world saw a seismic upheaval. The transaction shook the sport, but it also served to popularize hockey in non-traditional areas. Gretzky's influence in Los Angeles stretched beyond the rink; he became a cultural star and was instrumental in broadening the NHL's reach.

Gretzky accomplished astounding milestones as he proceeded to rewrite the record books. He broke Gordie Howe's long-standing record of being the NHL's all-time top scorer. His 92-goal season in 1981-82 maintains an unbroken single-season record.

Gretzky remained modest and team-oriented despite his own achievements. He frequently emphasized the value of team achievement above personal honors. His leadership and passion to his profession inspired teammates and aspiring hockey players all across the world.

Wayne Gretzky announced his retirement from professional hockey in 1999. He departed the game with an unrivaled legacy, including the most career goals, assists, and points. He was a 10-time scoring champion, a Hart Trophy winner nine times, and a Stanley Cup winner four times.

Wayne Gretzky's contributions to the sport extended off the rink. He was a successful coach and later worked as an executive for several NHL clubs. His influence on the growth of hockey in the United States and subsequent generations of players was tremendous.

The narrative of "The Great One," Wayne Gretzky, continues to inspire hockey players and sports fans all around the world. His path from a little Canadian village to hockey immortality exemplifies the transformational power of ability, hard effort, and an unwavering dedication to one's art. Wayne Gretzky's name will always be associated with success.ence in the world of sports.

What can we take away from Wayne?

Wayne Gretzky's incredible path teaches many key life lessons. His ability to predict where the puck would be rather than simply where it was highlights the importance of imaginative thinking. This talent, developed through hours of practice and a natural grasp of the game, highlights the need of strategic planning in both personal and professional endeavors.

Gretzky's success has also been defined by his consistency. His unrelenting work ethic, day in and day out, emphasizes the value of steadfast devotion. Achieving excellence frequently takes consistent effort and a dedication to constant growth.

Gretzky's famous adage, "You miss 100% of the shots you don't take," reminds us of the importance of taking sensible chances. Stepping outside one's comfort zone and grasping chances are frequently required for success.

Despite his unrivaled brilliance, Gretzky maintained a remarkable level of humility throughout his career, demonstrating that humility is a sign of real greatness. He emphasized the importance of collaboration and effort in attaining common goals over personal glory.

Another source of motivation is Gretzky's leadership on and off the rink. His ability to inspire and uplift his peers illustrates the power of inspiring leadership in any area.

Finally, Wayne Gretzky's everlasting impact, both in and beyond of hockey, reminds us of the value of making a lasting impression. His contributions to his sport, community, and the lives of others he inspired are proof of the long-lasting influence one may have.r chosen field.

"A good hockey player plays where the puck is. A great hockey player plays where the puck is going to be."

Gretzky inspires us to think beyond the present and anticipate future trends.

12

MICHAEL PHELPS

"I think goals should never be easy; they should force you to work, even if they are uncomfortable at the time."

Michael Phelps is the most decorated Olympian in history, with a record-breaking 23 Olympic gold medals in swimming. His remarkable swimming performances, including multiple world records, cemented his place as one of the greatest athletes of all time. Phelps' name is connected with swimming prowess and domination. Aside from his sporting abilities, he is also known for his activism for water safety and mental health awareness. Michael Phelps is admired not only for his unrivaled competitive achievement, but also for his services to society and honesty regarding personal struggles.

Michael Phelps: A Swimming Victory

There is no more distinguished name in swimming than Michael Phelps. His transformation from a little child with enormous hopes to the most decorated Olympian of all time exemplifies the power of devotion, resilience, and unshakable drive. Michael Phelps' narrative, sometimes known to as the "Flying Fish," continues to inspire generations across the world.

Michael Fred Phelps II was born in Baltimore, Maryland on June 30, 1985. His love of water was obvious from an early age. Debbie Phelps, his mother, saw his potential and enrolled him in swim classes when Michael was seven years old.

Phelps' skill began to flourish at the North Baltimore Aquatic Club, under the tutelage of his coach, Bob Bowman. Early on, his incredible work ethic and unrelenting pursuit of perfection were clear. Even as a young swimmer, he established a seemingly impossible goal for himself: to become the greatest swimmer in the world.

Phelps' Olympic career began when, at the age of 15, he qualified for the 2000 Sydney Olympics, becoming the youngest American male swimmer to compete in the Games in almost 70 years. While he did not win a gold, his appearance on the Olympic stage signaled the start of an incredible career.

Phelps emerged as a swimming phenomenon at the 2004 Athens Olympics. He took home six gold medals and two bronze medals while setting a new world record in the 400-meter individual medley. His performance in Athens pushed him to international celebrity and cemented his place in the public consciousness.

Despite his triumph, Phelps maintained his composure and continued to push himself. His quest for perfection extended beyond the pool, as he collaborated with his coach to fine-tune his technique and devise a rigorous training routine.

The 2008 Olympics in Beijing would prove to be the highlight of Phelps' career. He set a daring objective of capturing eight gold medals in a single Olympic Games, which had never been done before. Phelps was subjected to enormous criticism and scrutiny, yet his mental toughness and preparation were unwavering.

Phelps not only fulfilled his aim but also established many world records in the process, demonstrating unprecedented supremacy. His wins varied from the 200-meter freestyle to the 200-meter butterfly, demonstrating his versatility and unrivaled talent. Phelps' performance in Beijing cemented his place as one of the best athletes in Olympic history.

Phelps' trip was not without its difficulties. He struggled with personal issues such as despair and anxiety. He momentarily retired from swimming in 2014, wondering if he would ever return. He sought counseling, began on a path of rehabilitation, and triumphantly returned in 2016.

Phelps won five more gold medals to his collection in the 2016 Rio Olympics, bringing his total to 23 Olympic gold medals and cementing his status as the most decorated Olympian in history.

Phelps' influence went beyond the pool. He utilized his position to spread the word about water safety and the significance of learning to swim, particularly among youngsters. His Michael Phelps Foundation sought to encourage healthy and active lives while also providing opportunity for marginalized youngsters to learn to swim.

Phelps continues to promote for mental health awareness after retiring, sharing his personal experiences and urging others to get treatment when needed. His candor about his challenges helped to reduce the stigma associated with mental health disorders.

Michael Phelps' story continues to inspire people all around the world. His passion, resilience, and unwavering pursuit of excellence serve as role models for budding athletes and anybody pursuing their aspirations. His willingness to discuss mental health issues has prompted crucial debates and given hope to people going through similar struggles.

Phelps' transformation from a teenage swimmer with huge goals to a global superstar and positive change champion exemplifies the transformational power of enthusiasm, hard effort, and determination. His influence in the pool and beyond will live on as a source of inspiration for generations to come.

What can we take away from him?

We may learn from Michael Phelps that steadfast commitment, unwavering pursuit of goals, and the bravery to handle personal challenges, such as mental health, can lead to exceptional achievement. His narrative illustrates the necessity of resilience, adaptation, and the capacity to recover from adversity stronger. Phelps' activism for water safety and dedication to give back to the community demonstrate the importance of using one's platform for good. His transformation from a teenage swimmer to a global celebrity displays how hard effort, determination, and passion can turn goals into reality, motivating others to attain their greatest potential.

"If you want to be the best, you have to do things that other people aren't willing to do."

13

ROGER FEDERER

"I always believe if you're stuck in a hole and maybe things aren't going well you will come out stronger. Everything in life is this way."

There is a character in the world of tennis who transcends the sport itself, a virtuoso whose elegance on the court and grace off it have grabbed the hearts of millions. Roger Federer, dubbed the "Swiss Maestro," is more than simply a tennis player; he is an icon, a symbol of greatness, and an inspiration to aspiring sportsmen and others all over the world. Roger Federer's life and career are examples of the power of skill, hard work, sportsmanship, and unflinching commitment.

A Childhood Fantasy

Roger Federer was born in Basel, Switzerland, on August 8, 1981, to parents Robert and Lynette Federer. Tennis was the logical option in a region famed for its gorgeous alpine scenery and enthusiasm for the game, and his path into the world of sports began at an early age. Young Roger exhibited a special ability for the sport from the minute he picked up a racket.

Recognizing his talent, his parents offered consistent emotional and financial support in pursuit of his objectives. He moved to the Swiss National Tennis Center in Ecublens, Switzerland, as a youngster to perfect his talents and receive professional instruction. Federer's skill blossomed under the tutelage of his coaches, notably Peter Carter, who was important in his growth.

The Formative Years

Federer's rise from promising junior to professional phenomenon was distinguished by hard work and sacrifice. He went professional in 1998, and while success did not come easily, he worked hard to improve his game, learning from every triumph and failure. In 2003, he had his breakout year, winning his maiden Grand Slam championship at Wimbledon, overcoming the powerful Mark Philippoussis. It was the start of something incredible.

Tennis proficiency

Roger Federer's game has been described as "poetry in motion." His smooth movement around the court, excellent shot-making, and exceptional agility enabled him to dominate on all surfaces. He won a record 20 Grand Slam tournaments, including eight Wimbledon crowns, six Australian Opens, five US Opens, and one French Open.

But it wasn't simply his successes that won him supporters around; it was also the manner he played the game. Federer's sportsmanship, elegance, and humility were lauded alongside his accomplishments. Whether he won or lost, he showed unshakable respect for his opponents and a true passion for the game.

The Conflicts

Federer's tenure in tennis overlapped with that of two other tennis greats, Rafael Nadal and Novak Djokovic, resulting in some of the sport's most legendary rivalries. His fights with Nadal, notably on Roland Garros' clay courts, are legendary. Federer's resolve to win the

French Open, his sole Grand Slam, culminated in a remarkable triumph in 2009.

His duel with Djokovic demonstrated both players' mental and physical toughness. They pushed each other to their limits in tremendous battles, enthralling viewers all around the world. Federer's ability to stay a contender in the face of such stiff opposition demonstrated his persistent talent.

Injury and Recoveries

Federer, like every other athlete, had difficulties. Injuries, notably a nagging knee, threatened to end his career. Federer's fortitude, on the other hand, shined through during these hard moments. He had surgeries, went through rigorous rehabilitation, and made incredible comebacks, demonstrating that persistence and enthusiasm could overcome adversity.

Away from the Court

Roger Federer's charity efforts have made an influence beyond of the tennis court. In 2003, he founded the Roger Federer Foundation, which is committed to increasing education and healthcare access for underprivileged children. His determination to make a good influence in the lives of others reflects his personality and principles.

The Inspirational Legacy

Roger Federer's life narrative inspires individuals of all ages and backgrounds. His transformation from a little child with a dream to one of the greatest athletes in history demonstrates the power of skill, hard effort, and unshakable commitment. Federer's sportsmanship and humility remind us that genuine greatness is characterized not just by wins, but also by how one conducts oneself on and off the field of play.

Federer's legacy will be protected as he aged gracefully and continues to compete at the greatest level. His influence on tennis and the world of athletics stretches well beyond his extraordinary exploits. Roger Federer is a symbol of greatness, a role model for young sportsmen, and an inspiration to everyone who appreciate the beauty of the game and the tenacity of a real champion.

In a culture that frequently glorifies individual accomplishments, Federer's narrative reminds us that greatness is about how one uses one's position to make the world a better place. Roger Federer has truly become a global hero and a source of inspiration via his incredible career and philanthropic efforts.

What can we take away from Roger?

We may learn the ageless principles of elegance, humility, and sportsmanship from Roger Federer. His career is an example of pursuing greatness via steadfast devotion and hard effort. Federer's regard for his opponents, whether in victory or defeat, emphasizes the necessity of humility even in triumph. His continuing love of the game, along with his ability to elegantly overcome hardship, shows us the tenacity required to overcome adversity. Federer's dedication to make a positive difference through philanthropy reminds us that genuine greatness extends beyond personal accomplishments, and that we can utilize our success to uplift and inspire others.

"I've always been aware that the image you patiently construct for an entire career can be ruined in a minute. It scares you a bit, but that's the way things are."

CONCLUSION

We've gone on an incredible trip through the lives and careers of some of the world's best athletes. These individuals, who come from a variety of backgrounds and sporting disciplines, have not only made an indelible impression on their particular sports, but have also transcended athletics to become sources of inspiration for all of us.

As we consider the stories of these extraordinary athletes, we see a similar thread—a tapestry woven with strands of perseverance, passion, resilience, and unflinching commitment. Their experiences teach us that excellence is earned by unshakable devotion, hard effort, and a determination to give up in the face of adversity.

Each athlete's path has demonstrated the extraordinary strength of the human spirit. We have seen the triumph of desire and the pursuit of perfection, from Michael Jordan's humble origins to Serena Williams' supremacy of the tennis court. Usain Bolt's electric speed and Babe Ruth's iconic home runs have shown us that we can break records and redefine what is possible with determination and a burning desire to achieve.

However, it is not simply their athletic exploits that distinguish great athletes; it is their character, sportsmanship, and capacity to inspire others that truly distinguishes them. Roger Federer's grace on and off the tennis court, Khabib Nurmagomedov's tenacity in the face of adversity, and Michael Phelps' unrelenting desire to overcome personal obstacles are all examples of the characteristics that make great sportsmen not only champions but role models.

We discovered great insights that go well beyond athletics in our investigation of these athletes' lives. We've learnt the value of perseverance in the face of adversity, the necessity of discipline in attaining our objectives, and the relevance of giving back to our communities.

As we come to the end of this inspiring trip, let us remember the stories of these athletes as a source of inspiration and a reminder that greatness is within the reach of those who dare to dream, work relentlessly, and believe in themselves. Let us be encouraged to follow our own passions with zeal and to utilize our success to effect positive change in the world.

These athletes' experiences remind us that our potential is infinite, and the only actual boundaries we set on ourselves. Let us strive for excellence, conquer hardship, and leave a lasting legacy of inspiration for future generations, guided by their stories.

Made in the USA
Las Vegas, NV
04 July 2024

91849611R00066